The Two of Us
A Sister's Love

Faye Curtis

Dreams do come true!
Faye Curtis
2021

Copyright © 2021 Faye Curtis
ISBN: 9798590517046
Independently published

Scripture quotations from The Authorized (King James) Version. Rights in the Authorized Version in the United Kingdom are vested in the Crown. Reproduced by permission of the Crown's patentee, Cambridge University Press

All rights reserved. No part of this publication may be reproduced, stored in a retrieval system, or transmitted in any form or by any means, electronic or mechanical, including photocopying and recording, without the prior written permission of the author, except for brief quotations in reviews.

Dedication

I dedicate this book to my lovely sister, Kinda Leshette Gilstrap, and to my precious three granddaughters, Brynlee, Kambrin, and Tinsley. The bond between sisters is an unbreakable bond that no one can ever break. I have truly cherished every moment that I was able to spend with my sister. We may not have been twins but you could not tell us any different because we wanted to do everything together.

Did we have our moments when she made me mad or vice versa? Yes, but our love was stronger than any problems we could ever face.

To my Lovely Granddaughters

I love you with all my heart and want you to know that this book will help you get through those times when you just do not feel like being around each other. Remember that being sisters is a wonderful gift from God and that each moment spent together is so precious. Never let anyone come between you and always protect each other. I can't wait to see the beautiful young ladies you will become in life. Keep God first, dream big and accomplish all your goals.

Special Acknowledgement

Michele and Faye

When I told Michele Bertone-Buck I was going to write a book and be recognized as an author at a conference in April of 2021, she was so excited that she said, "Come over so we can get to work." I went over to her house and we started brainstorming book titles, business names, and different logos. She even said, "Oh, I can't wait to go to the book launch." Michele then asked if she could buy tickets in March of 2020 for next April 2021. She told me she would not miss it for the world. She was so proud of me.

Despite the fact that she was fighting her battles, that never stopped her from being my support system and encouraging me to continue to write. She loved some of my childhood memories and thought I should share them all.

Michele Bertone-Buck was an eleven-year cancer survivor who gained her wings on May 23, 2020. She was a wonderful best friend to me, and I am grateful for every day and moment I spent with her until the end.

I love you dearly, Michele, and I'm glad you are my guardian angel. RIH (Rest In Heaven)

Endorsement

Stacey and Faye

It is a huge honor to be writing an endorsement for my sister Fabrienne Curtis' first book. Sister bonds are some of the strongest relational bonds that exist. There are blood sisters, the ones that you share the same parents with, and there are your spiritual sisters, the ones that GOD places on your life's path. Sisters share advice and opinions on just about everything, from what outfit to wear to "Do think he's the one I should marry?" And yes, sisters have disagreements as well, but that should never stop the love that sisters have for one another. But if it does, it is that same love that will bring them back together and even closer than before. Sisters are the ones that you can be vulnerable to and never worry about being judged. When you have had the most horrible days ever and you just need to cry, guess who's there for you? You got it—your sister!

      Sisters encourage, empower, support, uplift and yes, they sometimes will check you, but that is what a real sister does. Sisters create lasting memories that are embedded in their hearts for a lifetime. Life is full of surprises, unexpected tragedies, and family disagreements that may take your sister from you, but GOD always places that right sister on your life's path. Hence, the godly sister. These sisters are no less important than a blood sister. God knows exactly what you need or who you need. He places that on your life's path. I believe everyone in your life is there for a reason, and the godly sister adds something a little different than what your norm is. Your godly sister will bring out those things deep within that you had no idea were even there. Maybe it is spiritual, that inner fashionista, or it could be a different way of viewing different life situations. As a result, I thank God every day for Fabrienne Curtis, whom I affectionately call my sister because we've been placed on each other's life path. We have been each others' heartbeats through life's ups and downs. God could not have given me a better sister. Never disregard those women who God has placed on your life's path, because they will bring or have what it is that you need to continue your journey.

    Sincerely, your godly sister,

    Stacey Scott Sr.

Endorsement

It is with great joy that I write this endorsement. Whether you have a birthright sister, or one who God placed into your life another way, this book is for you. Faye has captured the true meaning of sisterhood with the experiences she shared with her beloved sister, Kinda. Her experiences will "take you there." Your "there" might be joyous memories, or perhaps they are bittersweet memories. You will find yourself laughing out loud one moment and wiping tears the next. Faye truly takes us on a journey of adventures from childhood to adulthood.

My connection to Faye is through her loving mother, who I called Sister Witt out of respect, but with much love. Ironically, we became best friends who were just like sisters. Faye's sister journey reminds us to cherish every moment we have with each other.

Phyllis Jenkins Powerful Journey, Founder
PowerLift Stories Podcast, Host

Table of Contents

Foreword	13
1. The Manhattan Days	14
2. The Block and Carwash Days	16
3. School Days and Ice Cream	19
4. Coney Island	21
5. George of the Jungle	23
6. Playing with Dolls and Hairstyles	25
7. The Fish Market	26
9. Tap Dancing	27
10. The Jams and Concerts	28
10. Carnegie Recital Hall	30
11. Ashford and Simpson	41
12. Cooking with the Oven	42
13. Modeling with Bathing Suits	44
14. Playground Fight	45
15. The Big Move to Texas	47
16. Schools in Texas	49
17. Texas Sports	50
18. Summers in New York	54
19. Church	56
20. Summers in Georgia	58
21. The Butter Exercise	62

22. Boys	65
23. The Big Shock	68
20. Sisterly Love	79
21. Memories	81
22. The Matriarch	91
23. Writing in the Pandemic of 2020	99
Meet the Author	
With All My Heart	
Acknowledgements	
Before You Go!	

Foreword

We are going on a journey of two sisters who were inseparable. The love we shared was unconditional and beautiful. Kinda and I cried, laughed, played, and experienced every aspect of life together.

The relationship with our cousins was special and the adventures we went on over the years were incredible.

We had a phenomenal life together involving travel, school, summer vacations, plays, and chatting about boys. My mother and adult cousin Martha made sure that we got to experience all aspects of life. But all the fun, adventures, and vacations came to an unexpected halt caused by an event neither-of us could have ever imagined. Our lives were changed forever. So, hold on to your seats and let's take the magical journey together!

The Manhattan Days

Our younger years were the best because we lived in Manhattan, New York. Being born in such a big city was so fascinating. We had an apartment right by the water and could look out and see everything. The greatest part of life was that our mother worked at our nursery school. She would make sure that all of our birthdays were filled with lots of cake and ice cream.

Our favorite cousins, Nigel and Crystal, lived in New York as well. The four of us were close and enjoyed life together. I was the youngest one in the group, but that did not stop me from keeping up with everyone. It was a great adventure each-time we went to play at our cousins' house.

Nigel and Crystal had a dog named Steppe. Can you imagine walking a dog in the city? One day we were all playing, and Steppe got loose and ran around the building several times. We just knew we would be in big trouble if we did not get him back.

After several hours of him running around the building, he got tired and came back to us. We got lucky that time because we would have been in so much trouble if Martha knew we lost her dog. Martha would let us play outside until dark. Then she would make us come in to do our hair. Oh, how I used to love her greasing my scalp and combing our hair.

Nigel was such a great cousin that he wanted to make sure we girls knew how to take care of ourselves. He taught us how to protect ourselves with some self-defense moves. I still remember some of those moves to this day.

The Block and Carwash Days

As cousins, we had a pact that we would never let each other get in trouble. When we would go over to their house, Kinda and I would save up all our money and go to the candy store. Often my mom and Martha would give us money as well, and we would combine our money to get an assortment of snacks. We would then take all the different candies and put them in separate bowls. The candies included Boston Baked beans, Jolly Ranchers, Milk Duds, Now or Later and Lemonheads. Once in separate bowls, they would be placed on the bed and we would have a party. Our party would consist of all the different bowls of candy, soda, and dancing. We all loved to dance and act silly.

If we were going to play outside, it would be on the monkey bars and directly in front of the apartments. Lots of people played on the monkey bars or played basketball. It was fun to be outside because it seems everyone would come home from school and not be worried about homework. But, of course, my mom was going to make sure we did our work.

    I remember one time in particular we decided to have a neighborhood car wash, so we gathered all the kids from the neighborhood to join. We had our clothes, soap, but did not have any water. So, we came up with the bright idea to use the city water. This would consist of breaking into the water fire hydrant. We used a tool to turn it on. We were charging people to wash their cars with the city water.

    As you can imagine, that did not last very long. A policeman came by and asked, "Who turned the water on?" None of us answered. The officer got out of his car and got a tool to turn the water off from his trunk. He told us do not turn that water back on or we would be in trouble.

    Since we live on blocks in New York City, you would not see the same police officer twice unless he was assigned to your street. Therefore, we waited ten minutes and then our block car washing was back on. We washed cars probably for about an hour until another police officer showed up and turned the water off. He gave us the same speech as the other officer.

    Again, we waited ten minutes and proceeded with our car wash. After officer number three, we all decided that we had better stop before we got into big trouble. I knew that I would be okay because I was the youngest in the group. The older children would get in more trouble than me.

School Days and Ice Cream

Kinda and I loved to go to school. I was very fortunate to go to Hope Day Nursery School where my mother worked as a teacher. I loved having her there, and she always made me feel special.

I was born on Valentine's Day. Every year my mom went out of her way to give me a big birthday party and have a cake shaped like a heart. All my family and friends would come to my birthday party as well. Kinda and I went to PS 197 in Manhattan, a large building with no windows in the classroom. Can you imagine being in a school with no windows in the classrooms? It was different from any other school I had ever seen. PS 197 was just a few blocks down from our apartment. A group of us from our block enjoyed walking to school together every day.

After school, Kinda and I would stop at our favorite ice cream store on the way home. This ice cream store had the best ice cream. Our favorite was an ice cream sandwich, not like the ice cream sandwiches today. It was shaped in a circle with one top hard cookie, the ice cream in the middle and then the hard cookie on the bottom. The owner of the store knew us so well that he did not have to ask what we wanted. He had it ready when we entered the store. They just don't make ice cream sandwiches like that anymore.

Coney Island

Coney Island was one of the places we enjoyed going as a family to relax. It was like a private getaway from everything where we could just have good, clean fun. The island is a beach that has a boardwalk, a lot of games, food, and people holding all kinds of animals. I loved being in my bathing suit and getting in the water.

There were times we would go with my other cousins just to have fun. Every time family came to visit, we took them to Coney Island for entertainment. Most of our family could not believe that there was a beach in New York. People skated on the boardwalk, played loud music, and a man carried a big snake around his neck. Of course, my sister and I were afraid of snakes, so going to pet or even look at the snake was out of the question.

We loved playing the game to win a stuffed animal. I recall the game where we threw the ring on the bottle and also the one where you had to squirt the water in the hole to make the animal move to the top. There was great fun at Coney Island, and I will cherish every memory of it.

The Two of Us

Faye and Kinda at Coney Island

Our Mother, Pauline Witt

George of the Jungle

You are really going to have fun reading this chapter. If you are a cartoon fan, you probably remember George of the Jungle. George was famous for flying through the air and shouting, "Watch out for that tree!" He was swinging from tree to tree. Being the awesome children we were, my sister and our favorite cousins Crystal and Nigel decided to act out the scene in real life.

We came up with a plan to get a bunch of bed sheets and tie them together. We cleared everything out of the room so that when we went flying from one end of the room to the other, we would not break anything. The desired destination was a pile of blankets and pillows. We each took turns. When it was my sister's turn; she flew through the air shouting, "Watch out for that tree," and immediately missed the pillows and landed on the floor. The floor was concrete, so you can imagine the loud noise it made and how hard she hit it.

Instead of checking to see if she was okay, all we could do was laugh until we cried at her landing. Thank

God, she was not badly hurt, but did have a headache for a few hours. Since Kinda did not make the mark and land on the pillows, we quickly stopped that role-playing.

Playing with Dolls and Hairstyles

My sister Kinda and I were best friends. We loved doing everything together. Many times, people thought we were twins (not identical, but look-alikes). Laugh Out Loud!

My mom, dad and Martha would buy us all kinds of dolls. The specific doll that was our favorite was the doll with a button that would make her hair grow very long. If you wanted her hair short again, just roll the button the opposite direction.

Kinda enjoyed creating new hairstyles and then trying to duplicate them on me. She could come up with a new hairstyle in minutes, and it would be so fancy. Once we had our hair done, we could play dress up and walk around the house modeling. I learned how to braid and French braid from my sister and playing with my dolls. Girl time was fantastic with her because she was a great teacher.

The Fish Market

The fish market was one of my dad's favorite places to take Kinda and me. He had a friend that worked there and wanted us to learn all about the different types of fish. Little did my dad know this would change the whole aspect of my life when I got older. You see, at this fish market all the products were live and needed to be prepared for cleaning. Afterwards they placed them in the window slots for sale.

If you have been to New York, then you would know the fish markets have the most horrible smell you could ever imagine. The market not only has fish but lobsters, crabs, oysters, and all other seafood. Seeing what happens to the fish at the fish market and watching them clean the fish was not good for my stomach. Kinda was okay with watching the whole process, but I cried and wanted to go home. As a matter of fact, to this day I will not eat any seafood other than fish. My seafood days were over before they started.

Tap Dancing

Our mom was amazing! She wanted her daughters to experience all aspects of life. She decided to put us in all types of activities so we could develop different talents. One of those talents was tap dancing. Kinda and I accepted the challenge. Tap dancing allowed us to express ourselves and get all the energy out.

The Jams and Concerts

Listening to certain music just made me happy. So happy that I would want to play outside all day. We grew up in the era when the Jackson 5, LL Cool J, RUN DMC, New Edition and others were popular. We did not have to worry about any cuss words or music that degraded women. Let me take you back in time to those songs. Here are some of our favorites:

1. Candy Girl - New Edition
2. Mr. Telephone Man – New Edition
3. Is This the End – New Edition
4. I Saw Mommy Kissing Santa Claus – Jackson Five
5. Rock the Bell - LL Kool J
6. I Need Love – LL Kool J
7. Friends - Whodni
8. One Love - Whodni
9. Big Mouth – Whodni
10. Peter Piper – Run D.M.C

11. It's Like That – Run D.M.C.

12. My Adidas - Run D.M.C.

13. ABC – Jackson Five

When we were outside jumping rope or playing hopscotch, some of the above songs would be playing. We all joined in singing the songs. I remember when Michael Jackson and Diana Ross were in concert. White tennis shoes with their names printed on them were on sale to promote the concert. I wonder what happened to our shoes.

Music was just one of our favorite things in New York. Our mom also took us to several plays. One that I will always remember is the original *Wizard of Oz* stage play. It had all the original cast including Stephanie Mills, Dianna Ross, Michael Jackson and others. My sister and I were so blessed to have a mom who wanted us to experience life and have great memories.

Carnegie Recital Hall

One of the other talents that my mother wanted us to develop was playing the piano. My mom and dad brought us a Baldwin 1970 brown upright piano for us to practice on. We still have that piano to this day, and it works great. Occasionally, I play around on it.

My mom enrolled us in the Carmen Shepperd School of Music. Pauline Witt, our mom, was on the committee with other parents to help make this school a success. The teachers were Leona Little and Carmen Shepperd. Kinda and I loved them so much and enjoyed playing. We were practicing for a huge recital being held at the famous Carnegie Recital Hall in New York. This was a huge accomplishment for us.

I remember this experience like it was yesterday. The song that I played was "The Swing" by Michael Aaron. When I went up on stage, I made the mistake of looking into the large audience of people. For the first time, I experienced stage fright. I began playing the song and then suddenly forgot the rest of my song. I did the next best thing and made up the ending. Of course, the audience did not know the whole song, but my teacher and sister did. I took my bow and promptly exited the stage.

Kinda played the song, "Swinging in the Fairyland" by Flaxington Harker. She nailed it and played it so gracefully with pride.

Everyone played their solos. Then Mrs. Shepard gave out prizes. Kinda and I received the first prize for the service award. I still have the book. The photo from 1977 is the same photo that I am using for my own book. The article about both of us reads as follows:

Fabrienne & Kinda Witt

Fabrienne and Kinda are the daughters of Mr. and Mrs. Willie Witt.

Fabrienne is five years old and started here in fall. She has done very well in her studies. She loves to sing also. Fabrienne takes dance lessons. She has performed in many affairs. She attends the Hope Day Nursery School. She has been very active in the life of the school having participated in public affairs. Fabrienne graduated from Nursery School in June.

Kinda attends class 5-22-1 at P.S. 197 where she is an Honor Student and has received several commendations in her academic work. This is Kinda's third year at this music school where she has received her entire music education. She has always been an Honor Student. Kinda loves sports and has taken dancing lessons. She has made several professional dancing appearances in the City. Kinda will receive one of the outstanding progress Honor Prizes today to add to her other Honor Pin (1976).

We had two pages of relatives and friends who signed our book and congratulated us. If you visit New York, try to visit Carnegie Recital Hall; and hopefully, you will remember our story.

Carnegie Recital Hall
154 West 57th Street
New York, NY

Faye Curtis

PROGRAMME

I

GOD OF OUR FATHERS WHOSE ALMIGHTY HAND ..... Geo...
SING .... Jnk...
School Chorus
Leonard McKenzie - Accompanist

MUSETTE .... Bach
JAMAHL K. Evans

TWINKLE, TWINKLE LITTLE STAR .... Trad. Arry. Voss
Jason Joseph

THE SWING .... Michael Aaron
Fabrienne Witt

PETIT MARCH .... Burnam
Shelli Owens

WALTZ OF THE CHRISTMAS TOYS .... Leila Fletcher
Delarno Sterling, Jr.

WALTZ Op. 40 No. 1 .... Rolseth
Erin Scott

ROCKET TESTING .... Burnam
Jeffrey Phipps

CLIMBING .... McLachlan
Dwana Evans

FAIRYLAND MUSIC .... Ada M. Piaget
Carolyn McIntosh

MINUET — from "Don Giovanni" .... Mozart
Jeanne McIntosh

PROGRAMME

II

EVENING SONG OF THE KNIGHTS .... Fletcher
  James Cadle
IMPROMPTU, Op. 142 No. 2 .... Schubert
  Claire McIntosh
SUR LA GLACE .... Crawford
  Gloria Anderson
ASLEEP IN THE DEEP .... H. W. Petrie
  Hewie Bodden, Jr.
TAMBOURINE .... Rameau
  Robert Davis, Jr.
MINUET IN G .... Beethoven
  Cecelia Davis
MELODY IN F .... Rubinstein
  Leslie Phipps
THEME FROM THE SONATA IN A MAJOR .... Mozart
  Kelli Owens
SWINGING IN FAIRYLAND .... F. Flaxington Harker
  Kinda Witt
SONATINA IN C Op. 36 No. 1 .... Clementi
  Shannon Clarke

III

THE SINGING FOUNTAIN .... Burnam
  Lynell Plummer
THE BELLS .... John Williams
  Anita Williams
AVE MARIA .... Schubert
  Pamela Roberts
THEME FROM FINLANDIA .... Sibelius
  Laverne Rhaburn
MINUET IN F .... Mozart
  Keith Famous
ALLEGRETTO IN A MAJOR .... Haydn
  Isidra Hightower
SOMERSAULTS .... Dorothy Blake
  Daisy Jones
ALBUMBLATT "FUR ELISE" .... Beethoven
  Jean Wilson
SONATINA, Op. 36 No. 5 .... Clementi
  Marc Copeland

— INTERMISSION —

First Prize Winners of Service Award – 1977

FABRIENNE & KINDA WITT

Fabrienne and Kinda are the daughters of Mr. and Mrs. Willie Witt.

Fabrienne is five years old and started her music in the fall. She has done very well in her studies. She loves to sing also. She takes dancing lessons and has performed in many affairs. She attends the Hope Day Nursery School. She has been very active in the life of the school having participated in public affairs. Fabrienne graduated from Nursery School in June.

Kinda attends class 5-22-I at P.S. 197 where she is an Honor Student and has received several commendations in her academic work. This is Kinda' third year at this music school where she has received her entire music education. She has always been an Honor Student. Kinda loves sports and has taken dancing lessons. She has made several professional dancing appearances in the City. Kinda will receive one of the outstanding progress Honor Prizes today to add to her other Honor Pin (1976).

Journal Project Prize Winners – 1977

LEFT TO RIGHT (First Row) Jamahl Evans, Shelli Owens, Dwana Evans, Fabrienne Witt, Erin Scott, Delarno Sterling, Jr.
STANDING (Left to Right): Marc Copeland, Kinda Witt, Cecelia Davis, Laverne Rhaburn, Kelli Owens and Robert Davis, Jr.

FIRST PRIZE: **Fabrienne and Kinda Witt**

SECOND PRIZE: **Shelli and Kelli Owens**

THIRD PRIZE: **Robert and Cecelia Davis**

HONORABLE MENTION

FIRST RUNNER-UP: **Marc Copeland**

Jeffrey Phipps   -:-   **Leslie Phipps**

Faye Curtis

A Special Thank You

to the

PARENTS

of the

CARMEN SHEPPERD SCHOOL OF MUSIC

Please accept my warmest personal thanks for the excellent cooperation shown in our Journal project also for your kind thoughts and deeds shown to me.

JOURNAL COMMITTEE
General Chairman .... Project - Carmen Shepperd
Assistant Chairman .... Project - Leona Little

BOOSTER CHAIRMEN
Dr. Sylvia Roberts -:- Mrs. Hattie Penister

COMMITTEE
Ms. Jean Giddins -:- Mrs. Mary Hightower
Mrs. Pauline Witt

ALUMNI PRESIDENT
Mrs. Helen Murray

USHERS
Sharon Cox -:- Beverly Johnson
JoAnn Ephraim -:- Susan Willis
Hyacinth Daniel

Honorary Parent Sponsors

CARMEN SHEPPERD SCHOOL OF MUSIC

Mr. & Mrs. Byron Anderson	Mr. & Mrs. Leo Latty
Mr. & Mrs. Hewie Bodden, Sr.	Mr. & Mrs. Edmond C. McIntosh
Mr. & Mrs. Glenon Butler, Sr.	Mr. & Mrs. Leonard McKenzie, Sr.
Mr. & Mrs. Elliott Carlos	Mr. & Mrs. Charles S. Owens
Mrs. Juanita Copeland	Mrs. Hattie Penister
Mr. & Mrs. Richard Cox, Sr.	Mr. & Mrs. Nauford C. Phipps
Mr. & Mrs. Lewis Croom	Rev. & Mrs. James Plummer
Mrs. Myrtle Davis	Mr. & Mrs. William Roberts, Sr.
Mr. & Mrs. Robert Davis, Sr.	Mr. & Mrs. Olen Robinson
Mrs. Judi Evans	Mrs. Wilma Scott
Mr. & Mrs. David Eversley	Mrs. Darita Stephenson
Mr. & Mrs. Randolph Eversley	Mr. & Mrs. John Taylor
Mr. & Mrs. Ronald Famous	Mr. & Mrs. Hector Vargas
Ms. Shirley Francis	Mr. & Mrs. Otis Watts
Mrs. Jean Giddens	Mr. & Mrs. Lewis Williams
Mr. & Mrs. Leighton Hightower	Mr. & Lloyd Willis
Mr. & Mrs. David Jones	Mrs. Mozelle Wilson
Mrs. Ida Joseph	Mr. & Mrs. Willie Witt

Faye Curtis

Love and Heartiest Congratulations from...

PARENTS, RELATIVES AND FRIENDS

of

KINDA & FABRIENNE WITT

Fay Duboose Adams
Don Ashworth
Barbra Batiste
Matthew Bethea
Joseph Burns
Jimmel Bryant
Mr. Joseph Burns
Joseph Campale
Thaleintia Campbell
Hattie Carson
Gloria Colon
Mr. & Mrs. James Crawford
Jimmy David
Mr. & Mrs. David Dickson
Sammuel Edmondson
Edward Fadarok
Shederryod Field
Robert Fischer
Darrell Ford
Eugene Frazier
Sonny Frazier
George Gerbacia
Mr. & Mrs. Luis Gonzalez
Harold Green
Ruthie Green
Mr. & Mrs. G. Hawkins
Kelvin A. Hendericks
Walter Hogue
Mr. & Mrs. Johnny Hoptkin

Mario & Teresa A. Iazzetti
Luther Johnson
Mr. & Mrs. J. A. Johnson
Mr. & Mrs. Sullivan Johnson
Mr. Julius
Edward Krezynowek
Mr. & Mrs. William C. Kuclier
Brenda Lackson
Howard Lawrence
James B. W. Lee
Donald Lee
P. Leptich
Mr. & Mrs. B. J. Mack
A. Marinos
Mr. & Mrs. Robert Martin
Johnny Martin
Bertha McLain
Arthur Miles
Robert Miles
Eva G. Miles
J. P. Miller
Richard Miller
Willie Miller
Thelma Miller
James W. Mosley
Mr. & Mrs. Randy Murray
Gerald Myers
Mr. & Mrs. Tony Nasta
Evelyn Newton

Teacher's Photo of the Award

Ashford and Simpson

Our cousin, Ann was visiting from Georgia. One day Kinda, Ann, and I were walking to the store to purchase candy. Living in New York City, you never knew who you would see walking down the street. As we kept walking, my cousin started screaming and we didn't know what was wrong with her.

To our amazement, she had spotted Ashford and Simpson (famous songwriters) walking toward us. Ann finally got herself together, and when we got close enough, she asked for an autograph. They were very nice and polite as they gave us their autograph. Mr. Ashford kissed my cousin on the hand before he left. She was in complete shock. Ann stared at her hand and claimed that she would never wash her hands again. Kinda and I laughed at her so hard that our stomachs began to hurt. Ann felt this was the best visit ever.

So my question for you is, if your favorite famous singer kissed your hand, would you, too, refuse to wash your hand?

Cooking with the Oven

My mother was an awesome cook. She loved to prepare our favorite meals. My sister and I wanted to learn how to cook just like our mom. We had the play ovens and cook sets, but that was not good enough for us. The real oven in our kitchen was always a fascinating device to us. We wanted to use it just like our mom.

We decided that we would try to cook some canned goods. That's right. We put two cans of food in the oven without opening them. We turned the oven on and were totally surprised by the results.

My mom entered the kitchen and asked what we were doing. We were speechless, until a loud popping sound began coming from the oven. Yep, the two cans exploded in the oven. When she opened the door, the food went everywhere. As I recall this story, it sounds very funny. However, it was anything but, because we were in a lot of trouble. My mom was so upset with us. We received a spanking because my mom said we knew not to turn the big oven on. The moral of this story is that our parents really did know what was best for us.

Modeling with Bathing Suits

One of the best times Kinda and I had was pretending to be models and trying on different clothes. We would play dress up and practice new walks. The funniest part was trying to walk in my mother's heels. I'm sure every little girl has tried to walk in her mother's shoes and put on her clothes to feel grownup. Our modeling would consist of picking out three outfits and walking down the hall to the living room as a model. Our living room had plenty of mirrors, so we could see ourselves as we posed. One of my favorite things to model was my bathing suit. I dreamt one day of being a professional model showing off my bathing suits. We took a ton of pictures.

Playground Fight

It was nice to be able to go outside. We loved playing on the monkey bars, playing hopscotch or jumping double Dutch. We had many friends who lived in our apartment complex. However, there was a set of twins who did not like Kinda and me. One day, there were many kids playing outside and having a good time. The ice cream truck came by and we had our favorite ice cream sandwiches. There was a double-Dutch jump rope contest going on, and some of our friends asked us to join in on the fun.

The twins did not like that and wanted to make a big deal about it. The one sister came up to me and started yelling in my face. My sister walked up to her and said, "Leave her alone." The twin did not like that, so she began to fight. I'm not sure how long this went on, but I do remember our dad picking us up. He put my sister on one shoulder and me on the other. My sister was still swinging at the girl, but my dad kept walking.

We got into the house and my dad told us to go to our room, clean up and wait for him. My mom asked what was going on. Daddy explained what he saw, but my sister and I were not able to share our side of the story. I was crying in our room because I thought we were in trouble. My sister told me to stop crying because we did nothing wrong. She said she was defending me since the twin pushed me down.

This caused a big problem because my dad said we should have not hit the twin, but my mom defended us. She said, "The girl pushed her sister, and she was just protecting her."

Our parents argued for a while, and I lay next to my sister and cried myself to sleep. Kinda said, "don't worry I will never let anyone hurt you because you're my sister and I love you."

The Big Move to Texas

Our parents were not sure if moving to Texas was the right thing to do. My mother's sister lived in Texas. She was having her first child and my mom wanted to be there to help. Moving from the city to the country was a big decision. When our friends heard that we were moving to Texas, they were sad. Coming from New York, I thought that everyone who lived in Texas owned a ranch and rode horses everywhere. It was so hard to imagine living in a place where I had to have a horse to get everywhere.

Our friends and family had a block party for us, and it was so much fun. We had made lifetime friends, and our favorite cousins were still going to live in New York. We made our parents promise that we could come back every summer to spend time with our friends and family. They agreed, and we were excited because we would get to see our cousin Martha and family during the summer. Kinda created a school memory book for friends to write in before we left. She had a very special male friend. They talked almost every day, and they promised to write letters back to each other. Here are some of the comments from the memory book:

2 Good 2 Be 4 Gotten,
Remember M Remember E But most of all, remember me, Texas, Texas! Open the gates. Here comes Kinda and her family in super skates, Good Luck in Texas and keep your grades up.

Schools in Texas

Transitioning to our new school in Texas was a big adjustment for us; especially for me, because I had to wear bifocal glasses. Some of the students stared and some even made fun of me. I cried a lot because I did not experience that back home. But my sister reminded me of how beautiful a person I was and that she always had my back.

Teachers and students had a hard time with saying my real name, Fabrienne. So people started calling me Fab. Then one day everyone started calling me Faye. Kinda convinced me that it was not all that bad being called Faye. People had never heard her name before either, but it was much easier to say than my name.

It took some time to adjust, but we soon began to make new friends and meet new families. These new families were very kind and loving. It was refreshing to finally have people other than family that we could talk to and go visit.

Texas Sports

It seems to be a big deal in Texas to play sports. As a New Yorker, sports were not such a big deal. However, all that changed when my mom said we needed to get more involved and keep the tradition of trying new things. One of the best feelings in the world is to be a part of a team. Therefore, Kinda and I decided it was time to join in all the fun.

The first sport I played was soccer, but I quickly learned that it was not the sport for me. You see, in soccer you have to play no matter the weather. I was okay with playing until we played a game while it was pouring rain and the ball hit me in the face. However, I was proud to say that I tried it.

Kinda immediately tried out for flag corps and passed the tryouts. She really liked it because that meant she would have the opportunity to go to all the football games. It was so much fun watching her perform.

The other sport that I tried was volleyball. Oh, when I tell you this sport was so much fun, I loved it. I became so skilled at playing volleyball with a great serve of the ball that the team began to call me Hitler. It was a great feeling to be playing volleyball and be a part of a team.

    The best sport of all for both Kinda and me was running track. She was a lot faster than I was, but we made a great team with all the other girls. Kinda was given the nickname "Horse" because she used her long legs to run fast in every event. I remember my sister and I on the same team. I was always the second leg in the sprint relay, and she ran the last leg. It seemed that no matter if the other legs got behind, Kinda would always be able to catch up and win the match. We received several medals and ribbons.

    Before I played any sport, I would always recite the Psalms 23 to get me ready and prepared to play.
Psalms 23: 1-6 (King James Version)
"The Lord is my shepherd; I shall not want. He maketh me to lie down in green pastures; he leadeth me beside the still waters. He restoreth my soul: he leadeth me in the paths of righteousness for his name's sake. Yea, though I walk through the valley of the shadow of death, I will fear no evil: for thou art with me; thy rod and thy staff they comfort me. Thou preparest a table before me in the

presence of mine enemies: thou anointest my head with oil; my cup runneth over. Surely goodness and mercy shall follow me all the days of my life: and I will dwell in the house of the Lord for ever."

Quoting this verse calmed all my fears, helped me relax, and play my best game. As a young girl, I learned to find scriptures to memorize and use them in my time of need. I loved Bible drills and scripture challenges; knowing these scriptures helped me to apply the scriptures in my everyday life.

The Twins

The Hayes family, dear cousins of ours, lived in New York. They had twin children, and we felt it a special blessing to have them in our family. I loved how Mr. and Mrs. Hayes both taught me different things, from cooking to how to give the best massages. Mr. Hayes said he thought I would make a great massage therapist one day.

One of my favorite activities was to go to their house, helping babysit the twins and talking to their parents. Being around the twin girls was so much fun, and I got a taste of babysitting at an early age. It would not be fun if I did not have a partner in crime to help me watch them. I did have that person, and his name was Keith. The girls loved Keith, and he was very entertaining. We would do anything to assure the twins had fun. We made many great memories watching them. It's an experience which I will always cherish.

Summers In New York

The struggle was real moving from New York to Texas. We had more friends and family in New York than we did in Texas. Every summer we would visit our cousins. It was such an exciting time to see our family that we decided to split our time at different places. Kinda had a very special male friend. They wrote letters to keep in touch. He was very special to her and she loved him dearly.

During my visits back to New York, I still got the opportunity to babysit the twins with Keith. Keith and I had become best friends and pen pals. Once we were watching the twins and decided to go outside to play ball. Somehow, Keith twisted his ankle. We were several blocks from the house, so we all decided to carry him home. It was the funniest sight ever. All of us girls tried to hold on to him and make sure he did not put pressure on his leg. We would always make sure to have the twins back home before the streetlight came on at night, so they could get ready for bed.

Summers in New York were always a blast. When the summer visit ended and it was time to fly back to Texas, we were extremely sad. It seemed as if our summers flew by too fast.

Church

Since we moved to Texas, it was very important to my mom for my sister and me to be in church. Often we were in church all day and night because we attended several services. It was great to learn, but there were times we wanted to stay home. As young children, we had to adapt and seek to know God for ourselves. We were very inquisitive in Sunday school and youth group. Kinda and I began to make new friends at the church, and we joined the choir.

The choir was awesome. We began to sing solos. At first it was difficult, but the more we did it the better we got. There was a woman at our church who could sing without the music so well that it could blow your socks off. I wanted to be able to praise God that way with my voice one day. My mother was also a remarkably good singer and loved to sing in the choir as well. The choir had three great sopranos from the same family.

One of the greatest moments was when my sister went up to join the church. The sermon preached that day frightened me a little. I was nervous when my sister hopped up and went down the aisle to join the church. I joined church much later, but knew God was calling me to be his servant. The church had a big baptismal pool that had a beautiful colored stained glass with many colors. The scary part for me was thinking that I had to go under the water and then come back up. I just knew that I was going to drown. Now you're probably thinking that I should not have had those thoughts, but I did. All I could think of was all that water, and one preacher holding me.

Summers in Georgia

We decided to switch things up a bit and visit our grandmother in Georgia. Oh, how we loved our grandmother! She was our rock and always loved to spoil us. She also loved to tell us great Bible stories. She could recite the Bible backwards and forwards without ever looking.

It was very different from the summers in the city. My grandmother lived in the country where there was a lot of red dirt and plenty of woods. She had an outhouse for her bathroom, and we would cry every time we went out there. It was scary to us. I would always imagine snakes and other animals coming to eat me.

We had the best grandmother. She would feed us really well and watch wrestling with us. My grandmother would teach us about God, and she taught us to memorize the scriptures.

We had other cousins who lived in Georgia. When we came into town, we would all get together to play. Playing outside until it got dark was exciting back then, because we felt very privileged to be able to play that long.

One of our favorite meals that my grandmother would cook for us was hot biscuits with bacon, grits, and eggs. She would take the homemade biscuits, cut them in half and put them on a plate. Then she would melt butter in the pan. As the butter was melting, she would take the grape jelly and heat it up. Once the jelly was hot then she would pour it all over the biscuits. Talk about mouthwatering, I know your mouth is watering while reading this. Right?

There were three great memories of us being in Georgia that I would like to share with you. One day, all of us got sick. We had high fevers, so my grandmother took a sheet and cut it in half. Then she cut up an onion and put it in the sheet. Next, she tied the sheet to our neck, wrapped us up in bed and told us to go to sleep. It was very hard to go to sleep with that onion smell going up my nose, but she was not playing. She had her hickory stick ready to spank us if we moved.

The Two of Us

During another summer visit, our cousins came to see us at our grandmother's house. We discovered there was a mouse somewhere in the kitchen. One of my cousins was afraid of it, so he fixed his sister a plate and we all waited in the living room. He set a trap for the mouse to come out and get the cheese. My cousin sat down and proceeded to eat and then her brother yelled, "Mouse!" The cousin eating fell out of the chair, got up screaming and ran out the door. My grandmother did not find that funny, and the brother was in a lot of trouble.

The rule was we could play outside as long as we were back inside before dark. Kinda, Jessica and I decided to play a game of good and bad guys. I wanted to be one of the bad guys, but Jessica and Kinda would not let me. So, I ended up being the good guy and wore my Wonder Woman body suit. Kinda and Jessica went to hide so I could catch them. I was so upset with them but played along anyway. I looked everywhere and could not find them. When I finally found them, Jessica was sitting on the bank and I noticed something green was moving. Once I got a little closer, I realized it was a snake. Kinda started yelling, "Jessica run! It's a snake!"

We all ran so fast back to the house. The problem was that Kinda and Jessica wanted to kill the snake and got some matches from the house. I stayed back because I knew that was not a good idea. I explained to my grandmother what was going on, and she went down to the bank to get them. My grandmother told them that setting the snake on fire would also burn the woods down and cause a lot of damage.

Kinda and Jessica had to go out and pick their own hickory stick to get a spanking. Since I was her favorite, I did not get a spanking (smile). There was never a dull moment during our summer vacations in Georgia.

The Butter Exercise

I believe that every girl dreams of growing up, having a dream wedding and living happily ever after. We see these images on television and in the fairy tales. However, we had a different take on what we wanted to be like when we were older women. You see, Kinda, Jessica and I dreamed of being top-heavy. We wanted to have a D+ cup size, so that we could wear the cute tops and show them off.

While we were all visiting at our grandmother's house in Georgia, we decided to do something about our chest not growing. I do not know remember where we got the idea, but we thought that if we spread butter (yes, I said butter) all over our chests, that would help them grow. We went into the kitchen, took all the butter out of the refrigerator and spread it all over our chest. We laughed and modeled around with butter on our chests, saying please grow to a great big size. That was short-lived because my grandmother came back from the store, and the three of us got into trouble for using all her butter. Of course, she later laughed at us once we told her why we used all her butter.

I am sure that as you read this story, you wondered if the butter exercise worked, right? As a matter a fact, it was very successful. The three of us got a bigger cup size than we expected. Our family and friends said they wished they could be our size. If only they knew the pain it sometimes causes being so big. I have thought about getting a breast reduction, but feel that sometimes, elective surgeries are harder than imagined. I will just enjoy my triple-letter size and be grateful for the butter.

The next time you go into the grocery store and see a stick of butter, remember our story and have yourself a good laugh.

The Two of Us

Butter

Boys

Kinda and I always talked about how many kids we would have and planned how our weddings would be one day. Kinda always said she wanted a big family, and I wanted to have five children. We both loved school and hated to miss any days. We said that we were going to graduate college and become very famous one day. Kinda was very popular and had many boys who wanted to talk to her. I, on the other hand, wanted nothing to do with boys. I was known as the mean one growing up, except if you were my best friend. Laugh out- loud!

It was prom time and Kinda spent the full day with the Greer family getting her ready. The Greer family was very special to us. When we moved to Texas, they welcomed us and made us feel loved.

My mom and Mrs. Flo Greer became best friends. Kinda, Sharolette and I would hang out together. Sharolette's brother was taking my sister to the prom. Kinda wore a beautiful baby blue dress to prom and had the perfect date.

She graduated from high school and the college of her choice was Texas Women's University. She wanted to become a nurse. Kinda made lots of friends at college and had a great relationship with her roommate. When her roommate was pledging for a sorority and had to stomp all night as initiation into the group. Oh, the things I learned from watching my sister and her friends while at the university. We would pick Kinda up from college, so we could spend the weekends together.

The time came for my sister to get married, and I was happy and sad at the same time. I could not imagine not having her around or us hanging out whenever we wanted. She had a small intimate wedding at our pastor's home in Plano, Texas. We met them when we first moved to Texas and considered them as family.

There were times that my sister wanted me to come and spend the night at her house, but my mom would not let me. My mom told me that she was married, and I did not need to be spending the night there. I was very hurt by that because all I wanted was to go be with my sister. I just had to settle for her coming over to the house or us just hanging out and then me going back home before bedtime.

Kinda and her husband decided to start a family. It was so exciting that she was going to be a mom. In our family, we have several sets of twins on my mom's side and my dad's side of the family. We even have a set of quadruplets. The torch was passed to our generation, and we all wanted to see who would be the one who had a set of twins. Well, the ironic part was that Kinda had two boys who were not twins, but they were born on the same day of the week, same time, same number date, but a year and a month apart. That was so bizarre and different to see that happen. I loved being their aunt and helping her with the boys.

  The other unique event in our family was being born on major holidays. My mother was born on Christmas Day, and I was born on Valentine's Day. It was different having birthdays on major holidays, but my mom knew how to make it very special and fun.

The Big Shock

The school year ended, and it was time for summer vacation. My mom asked me if I wanted to go to New York or to Georgia. Since my sister was married and had a family, she was not able to go with me. This particular summer I wanted to go spend time with my grandmother, because we always had fun together. I loved going to visit my grandmother and grandfather. It was truly a blessing to spend time with them and my great grandmother. This summer was very different than most because my sister did not want me to go to Georgia. I told her it would be ok and that I would come back before the summer was over. Every day my sister called to talk to me on the phone, but that was not good enough for her. She even talked about how she missed our dad and that she wished he would come and visit us. Our dad lived in New York because he and my mom had separated.

All we wanted as girls was to be daddy's little girl and spend time with him. Kinda had a lot going on in her personal life and was having marital issues. She had once told me that she wanted a divorce and to move to New York, where her friends and family would help her start over. It was very upsetting to have that conversation with her, because I knew how she longed to be married. Sometimes life does not go as planned. A few days later, a carrier came to my grandmother's house and left a FedEx package for me. This was not common to get FedEx packages in my grandmother's neighborhood, because she lived in a very small town that was very far from the city. My grandmother asked me if I was expecting a package, and I said, "No ma'am."

I opened the envelope, and inside was a one-way plane ticket to Texas for the next day. I was so devastated. I immediately called my mom crying and asked her why I had to return home early. My mom said she did not send a ticket for me to come home. I immediately knew who did it. I asked my mom if I could please speak to my sister.

She got on the phone, and I said, "Why did you buy me a plane ticket to come home?"

Kinda replied that she missed me and wanted me to come home to spend time with her. I replied, "Okay, you win, since you went through all the trouble to pay for my plane ticket and FedEx it to me. Goodnight, love you. I'll see you tomorrow."

I spent the rest of the day enjoying my grandparents and getting packed to go home. My grandparents took me to the airport, and I told them next time my visit would be longer. I did not get to say goodbye to my other family members, since it was such short notice of my leaving.

My sister picked me up from the airport and gave me the biggest hug as if she had not seen me in years. I told her, "You know I am upset with you, but I love you so much and I am here for you."

We left the airport, and we went to the mall to hangout and have girl time. Kinda and her husband were spending the night at our house, and my nephews were visiting their other grandmother. We were like two little kids having fun at the mall trying on different outfits and bonding. Kinda talked my ear off, and I did the same to her. It was great because we were together and had each other's back.

Before we left the mall, we tried to call our dad so we could chat with him, but we did not get a response. Kinda said she wished our dad had time for us and explained to me how much she missed having him around. I tried to change the subject because it was a very painful topic for both of us. My mom took care of us the majority of the time after my parents separated.

We spent the entire afternoon together, but now it was time to go home to visit with everyone. When we arrived home, Kinda's husband was making spaghetti for dinner. We had a nice dinner and watched a few good movies with our mom. I expressed to my sister that I was glad that we all spent family time together, and I loved her. We watched one final movie, but towards the end Kinda complained that she had a headache and was ready to lie down. We stopped the movie, I said goodnight, and we all went to bed.

I am not sure what time it was, but all I could hear was Kinda's husband screaming for us to come into the living room because he could not wake my sister up. She was lying there peacefully on the bed. My mom immediately dialed 911, and I ran outside to watch for them to come.

While I was on the stairs waiting for the ambulance to come, God showed me a vision that my sister was already gone and was now with Him. I was sixteen years old at the time, very much afraid, and did not fully understand why God was giving me this vision.

The ambulance arrived. They asked if she had taken anything before bed because she had red stuff coming out of her mouth. I said we ate spaghetti for dinner and that was all. They were trying to work on her in the house. I stayed outside and prayed.

Kinda was rushed to the hospital, and we followed behind them. There was so much going on. I was in complete shock and could not believe this was happening. I do remember my mom's best friend and other family coming to the hospital.

Finally, they came and told us that my sister had an aneurysm that had raptured and that there was no brain activity. She could only stay alive with the use of the life support machine. Hearing that at that moment made me sick to my stomach. I asked if I could go be with her now. The doctors said yes, but they were waiting on a decision. Since she was married, the decision was up to her husband and not my mom, which made me angry. I could not understand how a decision as important as this one could be made by one person and not another family member. I just wanted my sister back, and I felt like the doctors needed to be doing more to save her.

Then God reminded me of the vision He had shown me earlier. However, I was in my feelings and could not discern or interpret the vision. All I knew was that my sister was slipping away. I went into the room to see her. There were so many machines connected to her. She made no movement, and this really scared me. This was the first time that I saw her lifeless and not talking to me. I could not even imagine how my mom felt or what was going through her mind.

The doctor came back and asked the family if we had made a decision about my sister. I could feel the tension in the room. Of course, we had people from church at the hospital praying and being strong for our family. Someone had called my dad, and he was trying to get a flight to Dallas.

Kinda's husband made the decision to turn the machine off at noon, which was only in two hours. All I was thinking was how did we get here? How is it so easy for you to say turn the machine off without making them check for more brain activity? I broke down crying and could not believe what I was hearing. He did not even ask the family what we thought or felt about the situation.

In less than two hours, I had to say goodbye to my sister, my best friend and the one person in the world I thought would grow old with me. We were supposed to share our lives together and watch each other graduate from college. We also wanted to become successful business women. This all seemed like a bad dream, and I wanted to wake up.

The time had come to turn off the machine. I was screaming and crying. I remember one of my sister's friends coming to hold me up and take me to another room, but I did not want to leave. It was too much for me, and I passed out in the hallway of the hospital. When I came to, my mom was standing there holding my hand and praying.

I did not want to go back to the house because that is the last place that I had seen my sister alive. It did not feel right for me to be there without her. I stayed at the house of one of my cousins, and my mom came with me. The hardest thing I had to do was say goodbye. I had felt pain before, but this type of pain was unreal and hard to bear. This was the first time I had ever had an anxiety attack. They told me that I had to calm down and not let this stress me out. I just kept crying to God and asking him, "Why now?" I was not ready for her to leave me yet.

All my family came in town for the funeral. We had an aunt who liked to dress everyone in the family who passed away. She wanted me to go with her to the funeral home and dress my sister. I told her there was no way that I could do that. I told her that I would pick out her favorite outfit and get it ready for her.

My sister loved her wedding dress and had told me if anything ever happened to her that she wanted to be buried in it just like a bride going to see her groom, who is Jesus. I found her wedding dress and got all the things ready so she could be a beautiful bride.

    My aunt did a great job of getting her ready for the funeral. I was not used to going to wakes, but I knew I had to do it for my sister. Just like every family, funerals bring out the worst in people. There were some people who came to the viewing who had no business being there because they made it very clear when my sister was alive, they did not like her. I was polite to them but made sure that they did not get anywhere near my sister. I could not understand why someone would take time out of their day to come to a viewing if they did not have anything to do with that person.

    The funeral was the most beautiful funeral that I had ever seen. One of her favorite male artists sang a beautiful solo and a lot of family and friends came from out of town. I felt so much love from everyone that it was overwhelming. My dad had come and brought me several gifts to try to ease my hurt and pain. But I was not happy with him at all. I told him that my sister really wanted to talk to him, and he never returned our calls. He was very apologetic, but I told him it was too late, because my sister was gone, and she could not hear his apology.

The funeral was a beautiful memorial service for Kinda. Lots of people came to pay their respects. I, on the other hand, was not doing well. I was hurt, confused and still in shock. I did not want to be around anyone. I just wanted to be alone. All I could do was cry and ask God, "Why now?" The more I reached out to God, the more I wanted Him to show me the way. I wanted Him to show me how to go on without my best friend.

One rainy day my eyes were open to the truth. I totally forgot that God had shown me a vision of my sister already passing before the ambulance even came, and that now she was with Him. It was scary trying to visualize that He was preparing me for that moment. I began to understand that God does not make any mistakes, and although I was being selfish and wanted her here, His plan and way are always best.

If we had left my sister on a life support machine, she would have been in a vegetative state. I had to ask myself if I would want to be connected to machines to keep me alive. I asked myself if I would want to be in a state of not being able to eat, talk or know my family. The answer was no. I know that God has a plan for our lives, and that we all must die one day. I just did not think that at the age of twenty-one, my sister would leave me. I had to do some soul searching. I asked myself, "If the shoe were on the other foot, and I had passed away instead of my sister, what would she do?"

We had talked about life and all the things we wanted to accomplish, but most importantly how we would serve God. I am going to be very honest: this loss was so hard for me. I knew that the only person who could get me through it besides my family would be God. I was going to have to let God minister to me and help me push through this pain.

So I decided to journal and write down a plan for my life. I wanted to make my sister proud and to accomplish my personal goals. I knew that God loved me and was not going to leave me alone. I had to rely on Him and His word to strengthen me in this time of loss. God's Word says he would never leave me nor forsake me. I had to read scriptures and recite them when I felt those weak moments coming up in my life.

I was determined to be strong for my sister and take care of our mom. I could not even imagine the pain that my mother was feeling. Losing a child so early in life had to take a toll on her, but my mom was so brave and strong. She never gave up on God or even questioned His will or way. That was all I needed to understand to help me keep my promise of moving forward with my life.

If you have ever lost a loved one, then you know the pain that I felt from this loss, but I want to tell you that God is awesome. Here is a scripture that helped me get through my loss. Lean on God and let him restore your pain to comfort.

17 The righteous cry, and the Lord heareth, and delivereth them out of all their troubles.

18 The Lord is nigh unto them that are of a broken heart; and saveth such as be of a contrite spirit.

19 Many are the afflictions of the righteous: but the Lord delivereth him out of them all.

20 He keepeth all his bones; not one of them is broken. Psalms 34: 17-20 (KJV)

I also listen to praise music to help give God the glory and keep me grounded in His word. Listen to the song, *I Need You to Survive* by Hezekiah Walker. It will truly bless you and keep you focused on the positive.

Sisterly Love

I had no idea that later on God would bless me with other women in my life that I would be able to call sister. God knows what we need when we need it. His timing is always perfect. We just have to trust his will and be patient. As I walk through this journey called life, God is showing me that even though He took my only blood sister, He was going to replace her with so much more. Over the years, He started with one, two, three, and then gave me sixty more sisters. God says that he will never leave you nor forsake you. I am a true witness to this statement. God gave me women who are sisters in Christ that I can call and depend on.

I know that loss is hard and we feel like we cannot go on, but look at God. I went from losing my sister at an early age to having more sisters than I could ever imagine. They are here for me through thick and thin.

You need to have some sisters in your life who are not afraid to be real with you. Sisters who will counsel you in the wee hours of the night, pray for you in your time of need. Sisters who are always willing to tell you the truth no matter how bad it is going to hurt. This type of sister does not have to be a blood relative. She can be whomever God places in your life. Whomever He trusts to fill that void of a missing sister in your life. Always be willing to trust God in the process because He knows what we need before we even say it or ask it.

    The biggest group of sisters I have gained over the years is my Pink Soles in Motion sisters. Our team consists of sixty team members, and I love them all. Our team does the three-day, sixty-mile walk for the cause to cure cancer. When I joined the team, Michele Bertone-Buck took me under her wing and showed me the ropes. My team is remarkable, and I love all these women. Next year I have determined to walk 120 miles in honor of Michele and everyone else who is battling cancer. God bless you all.

Memories

Michele and Faye

Pauline, Faye, Kinda

Kinda and Faye

Kinda and Faye

Faye, Santa, and Kinda

Pauline and Kinda

Stacey and Faye

Faye Curtis

Faye and Jerry

Faye with Sons Jeremy and Joshua

Kinda, their mother Pauline, and Faye

Faye and Pauline

The Matriarch

Pauline Witt meant a lot to billions of people, but to me she will always be my mother. I chose the above photo of her, because it reminds me that she was a warrior for the Lord. She said, "For God I live and for God I die." She was the greatest example of what God's true love felt like and she was even born on Christmas Day. There was not a day that went by that she did not give God the glory for all the things He had done in her life.

I recently lost my mom to a disease that takes most people by surprise and they give up. My mom, on the other hand, had told me she was going to do this her way. That is what she did. I remember times when the doctors would tell me that she was not going to make it, but God had another story in mind for her. I thank God for the Powerful Journey Organization, because through it, my mother's story is published.

Her book,
The Vision: How God Saved My Life,
is sold on Amazon.com.

One of her proudest moments was getting to tell her story in front of hundreds of people at the Powerful Journey Women's Conference. Being a part of the Powerful Journey was a blessing for her, because she got to work with her best friend, Phyllis Jenkins. Traveling to other states sharing her story and being a witness gave her great joy. Even when she was not able to travel on her own, she made sure her story was going forth and God would get the glory.

My mom was the nurse in the family. Everyone knew they could count on their Aunt Pauline to give them a remedy for what was ailing them. If she could not give them a remedy, she would read healing scriptures and pray. She was an astounding prayer warrior. My mom also loved to sing praises to God and sing in the choir. She wanted to sing with our church choir, but did not get the chance, and that is okay.

I am sharing with you about my mom because I need every reader to know that losing a loved one, whether it is your mom, sister, brother or others, it will be okay. God is always in charge. My mother told me that if God did not heal her on this side of earth, He would heal her on the other side. Was it hard for me to say goodbye to my mom? Absolutely, it was hard. Do I miss her dearly? Yes, I do.

Glory to God, she was saved and healed. You see, I know beyond a shadow of doubt that my mom is my angel looking down on me smiling and rejoicing.

She is doing all that because her daughter gets it. Her daughter knows that God and Mom were preparing me for this time. They want me to carry on with spreading the good news of the gospel of Christ.

In my mom's final hours, I got the opportunity to witness to her and sing praises to God. I walked in the room and played one of her favorite prayers by Cindy Trimm. I expressed how much I loved her, and that it was okay for her to go be with the Lord. She passed in her sleep and had a smile on her face. It reminded me of how her mom (my grandmother) and my sister both passed peacefully in their sleep as well.

Now I know what it meant when my grandmother used to say someone was always praying for me, and I will be stronger because of it. God made us a promise that He would never leave us nor forsake us. He is the one person who loves us unconditionally and will *never* hurt us! Trust and lean on his understanding, and I promise you that the pain of losing family members, friends, co-workers etc. will get easier with time. You cannot stay in that negative place and keep dwelling on what happened. I am not saying *not* to grieve, but do not let the grief consume you. Hold onto God's Word and get positive people in your life who will lift you up and walk alongside you.

As you are moving through this transition of a loss in your life, say to yourself, I AM A SURVIVOR!

Here are the things you can survive when you put God first and have positive people in your life. Say these affirmations daily:

- I can survive loss!
- I can survive heartache!
- I can survive challenges of life!

Then read the following scriptures:

Psalms 27:14 (KJV) Wait on the Lord: be of good courage, and he shall strengthen thine heart; wait, I say, on the Lord.

1 Thessalonians 5:8 (KJV) But let us, who are of the day, be sober, putting on the breastplate of faith and love; and for an helmet, the hope of salvation.

1 John 5:14 (KJV) And this the confidence that we have in him, that, if we ask any thing according to his will, he heareth us:

Philippians 4:13 (KJV) I can do all things through Christ which strengtheneth me.

This Prayer is for You

Dear Heavenly Father, bless the person who is reading this book. If they have had any type of loss in their life and are still hurting, Father, I ask right now that you remove all the hurt and pain. Lord, fill their heart and mind with pleasant memories and thoughts. Let them know that You love them and sent Your only Son that they might be free. If they do not know You for themselves, Lord, I ask that You touch them in a special way. Let them ask, "What must I do to be saved?" and confess that You are Lord and Savior over their life. Order their steps, Lord, that they have a prosperous life and come to truly know and feel Your unconditional love, in Jesus' name I pray, amen.

If you want to accept Jesus Christ as your savor, it is simple. God's Word says in Romans 10:13 (KJV) "For whosoever shall call upon the name of the Lord shall be saved. "So if that is you. when you are ready, say the following prayer out loud:

Prayer of Salvation

"Dear God, I want to be a part of Your family. You said in Your Word, that if I acknowledge that You raised Jesus from the dead, and that I accept Him as my Lord and Savior, I would be saved. God, I now say that I believe You raised Jesus from the dead and that He is alive and well. I accept Him now as my personal Lord and Savior. I accept my salvation from sin right now.

Now, I am saved! Jesus is my Lord. Jesus is my Savior. Thank you, Father God, for forgiving me, saving me, and giving me eternal life with You. Amen!

I included the scriptures and prayer because it is so important to have a foundation and covering over your life. You have to know that you know where you are going when you leave this earth. We all have an expiration date. Don't let it come and you not have Jesus Christ as Savior in your life.

Pauline Witt, thank you for being the rock in my life. I salute and honor you for installing in me values and God's way. You have passed the torch on to me, and I gladly accept the challenge. I promise to be the daughter you wanted me to be and inspire, motivate, and share the gospel of Christ every day. I will make you proud on the stage during my book launch and will dedicate all my speeches in your honor. I will always love you, Mom, and I can't wait to see you again.

Writing in the Pandemic of 2020

The thought of being a published author never crossed my mind until after the passing of my mother. It was at that very moment God spoke to me and said, "You do have a story to tell and you to need to get your book out there." I never realized the true impact the Powerful Journey Organization had until I remembered all the wonderful things my mom and Mrs. Phyllis had done together. It was as if my mom was saying, "Now you finally get it. I want you to carry on what I have started."

I agreed to take this journey, but never in my wildest dreams would I imagine it being like this. The pandemic hit and all of our lives are being been affected. Out of concern and caution, our Authors Academy is meeting virtually. It has been different and sometimes difficult, but we have managed. We went from being able to go to work, church, and shopping to being in quarantine for months.

Nothing about writing a book during a pandemic is normal. However, I have pushed through to get it done.

After working from home, I would log out of work and then write content for my book. This has been one of the most difficult tasks I have ever had to accomplish. Some days after work, I had to force myself to get back on my computer to work on my book.

There were days when I would rather relax than write. Commitment, dedication and drive became my companions. Honestly, there were days when doubt would set in. I would hear words like, "You are never going to become a published author. Do you really think you can write a book during a pandemic?" It seemed like the more I was home working, the more issues came about at work that demanded more of my time. I thank God that He is the head of my life, and I can call on Him when times are hard.

I had to let go and let God help me with all the fears. There were some days God would wake me up and remind me of certain parts of my life that I needed to add in my book. I would roll over and add them to my note section in my phone. I often keep notes in my phone when a memory came to mind that needed to be in the book.

The class taught me to write down what I needed to accomplish the following day, and make sure that it happened. One of the best parts of being on a team is our Members Only Facebook Group, as well as the GroupMe chat. I loved how on Fridays in our Facebook group, Mrs. Phyllis would post "Let's Celebrate your WINS for the week." That was so encouraging because it gave us something to strive for. The whole group would comment and celebrate the wins together as a team.

Through the GroupMe, we could also chat and encourage each other on a daily basis. Once a month we had our Authors Class via Zoom due to COVID-19. One of my favorite techniques that we learned in the class was to imagine a person sitting in front of you. This person was anxiously waiting for you to finish writing your story. I could literally sometimes envision a person sitting with me in my office saying, "I want to hear your story; keep writing until you are finished."

Learning that gave me so much writing power, because I know that my story is going to bless someone. The Powerful Journey Organization also had us do accountability calls once a month to check in and see if we needed any help. Just knowing that they are so caring and are cheering us on to get finished is profound.

Let me change gears for a moment. Allow me to share some of the unpleasant moments of writing during this pandemic. The more I wrote about my past, the more memories come to mind that I had suppressed. Many of these memories I had not thought about since I was a little girl. Sometimes I would succumb to my emotions and could not stop crying. I even at one point questioned myself if I even wanted to share some of those memories that were so painful for me to remember. These times were worse for me because I have recently lost my mom, and I could not ask her about some of the memories. I wanted to ask her why they hurt so much. The accountability calls were a great help because I immediately learned the resurfacing of these emotions was normal. I believe being stuck at home made it worse for me.

The moral to this chapter is that you should not let anything stop you when you are determined. Sometimes your journey may not be easy and trials will come, but remember that you can accomplish anything that you set your mind to. All it takes is determination, drive, prayers, willpower and positive influencers in your life. Set your goals and dreams. Celebrate your weekly wins no matter how small or big. I honestly believe that everyone has a story to tell and it could change the course of another person's life, but you have to be willing to do the work to get your story into the world.

Meet the Author

Faye Curtis is a wife, mom, grandmother, sister and a daughter of the King. She is passionate about encouraging and helping others become the very best person God intended for them to be. Through Faye's eyes, all lives matter because God created them in His image to be like Him. Faye enjoys being church secretary for Pastor Mike Owens, Sr. at Disciples of Christ Bible Fellowship. She has accomplished several personal goals and completed her MBA/TM in 2014, two years earlier than her personal goal timeline.

Helping and inspiring teens to achieve their goals is one of many missions in Faye's life. Students on Service

(SOS) exists to help at-risk youth. The program averages 500 students per year. These students are referred from the court for various offenses they have committed. The program reaches into the community to help, but also to help develop the students who come through the court system. Faye started in a volunteer capacity devoting her Thursday nights and Saturdays working with the students and parents, and she has been the director of the program. Faye is a liaison with community leaders, businesses, and non-profit organizations.

She has been instrumental in the 98% success rate with the students and the over 500,000 hours of service given back to the community. Faye is always early to events, classes, and meetings. She pays great attention to detail and makes sure that SOS is compliant with local, state, and federal laws.

Faye is also committed to walking sixty miles or more each year until there is cure for breast cancer. This type of passion is truly a blessing. If you would like some inspiring affirmations for your life, connect with Faye Curtis for a one-on-one session at **www.fayedivineinspirations.com**

Remember, if you dream it, you can achieve it!

God bless,
Faye Curtis

With All My Heart

♡

To My Lord and Savior:

Thank you, Lord, for ordering my steps and helping me with this vision. I love you dearly, and I'm proud to be a daughter of the King.

Lord, please bless everyone reading this book. May they come to know Your powerful love.

Acknowledgements

My heart is so full right now. All the love and support that I received writing this book was amazing. I would like to thank my husband, Jerry Hardeman, for his encouragement and support. I love you, babe. I want to thank my sons, Joshua and Jeremy, for loving me through this whole process and being your mom's biggest cheerleader.

To all my family, friends and sisters: Thank you for supporting me on this new journey of becoming an author. I could not have done it without you.

A special thank you to Martha and Crystal for helping make the childhood memories special and continuing support me.

To My Pastor and First Lady Michael and LaQuetta Owens: Words cannot express how deeply grateful I am for all the prayers, support and encouragement. It is truly an honor to be a part of such a loving church family. I love you both dearly.

Before You Go!

Please share your thoughts with friends

- Write a review on Amazon.com
- Connect with Faye Curtis at

www.fayedivineinspirations.com

- Connect via email:

faye.divineinspirations@gmail.com

- LIKE- Divine Inspirations by Faye on Facebook, and please share a comment when you read The Two of Us

Made in the USA
Middletown, DE
07 April 2021